MISSING PIECES,

CREATING THE LAURA'S

DASH SERIES

OTHER BOOKS

by Sharon S Darrow

Bottlekatz
A Complete Care Guide for Orphan Kittens

Faces of Rescues;
Cats, Kittens & Great Danes

From Hindsight to Insight,
A Traditional to Metaphysical Memoir

Tom Flynn, Medium & Healer

Navigating the Publishing Maze,
Self-Publishing 101

She Survives, Laura's Dash Book 1
Strive and Protect, Laura's Dash Book 2
Desperate Choices, Laura's Dash Book 3
Her Triumph, Laura's Dash Book 4

Short stories appear in the following Anthologies:

Lizard-Love, in *Birds of a Feather*
Introduction to Chickenese, in *More Birds of a Feather*
Travel Means Flying, in *Destination, The World, Volume 1*
First Solo Trip, in *Destination, The World, Volume 2*
Hanukkah Paper, in *All Holidays 2020*
Mothers' Day Surprise, in *All Holidays, Volume 2*
Born 100 Years Too Late, in *Volume One, Beautiful Americas 2022*

MISSING PIECES,

CREATING THE LAURA'S

DASH SERIES

SHARON S DARROW

SAMATI PRESS

SACRAMENTO, CALIFORNIA, USA

The material in this book is a true account of the creative process of the four-book. series that make up the Laura's Dash Series, most importantly, the reasons why certain characters and events were designed and included in the narrative. If any of the made-up characters or events resemble actual people or events it is purely coincidental.

First Edition 2024
ISBN 13 — 978-1-949125-42-9 (Print Version)
ISBN 13 — 978-1-949125-43-6 (Digital Version)
Library of Congress Control# 2024939317

Edited by Black Cat Editing Service
https://blackcatediting.weebly.com

Publisher: Samati Press
Sacramento, California
Manufactured in the United States of America

Dedication

This book is dedicated to a very special woman named Marlene Meincke. She started out as a coworker turned good friend to my husband when they both worked for the Small Business Administration Disaster Reserves. Then Marlene and I met and formed our own friendship, which blossomed in a new direction. Like me, Marlene is a voracious reader and was willing to try serving as a ~~Beta~~ Beta reader for each of the four books in the Laura's Dash series. She not only did a good job noticing little things that needed fixing, but was helpful and supportive throughout the process. So, to Lady Marlene, precious friend and valued Beta reader, thank you for being you. We think the world of you and are so grateful to have you in our lives!

I'm also dedicating this book to my first-born daughter, Shelley Ann Young, who passed away much too early on March 21, 2024. She fought colon cancer for two and a half years but lost the battle at only fifty-four years old. It hurts so much to lose a child, and seems so wrong to outlive them, especially one who was so full of life and love. Heaven is a ~~a~~ richer place with her, but it still seems wrong.

INTRODUCTION

Spoiler Alert

This book will reveal many of the key events that take place in the four books of the Laura's Dash series, as well as more information on characters, both factual and fictional. To avoid having important plot incidents revealed, you should read those books first.

If, however, you are one of those readers who likes to peek at the last chapter and then watch for all the little hints on the way (like I do), read on. You might even enjoy the inside information about which characters were made up and see if you think the author did a good job of giving them enough background and depth.

Sneaking a look at the end of a book is one thing, but with this four-book series, you might prefer reading this book in sections that correspond to the individual books while your memory is fresh.

Whichever type of reader you are, I hope you enjoy this in-depth look at the evolution of the Laura's Dash series.

CONTENTS

Book One,

She Survives

Chapter One

A “HALF-BREED”

Laura Cavanaugh Webber Wagner was the central character of the four-book series, Laura’s Dash. The word "d~~D~~ash" refers to the dash on a tombstone between the birthdate and date of death. That dash sums up the person's whole life. The poem, *The Dash* by Linda Ellis, explains the meaning of that dash beautifully. I wanted to put it at the front of each book, but the cost was way out of my reach. The Laura in this series was based on Laura Sullivan Turner Schomaker, known to me as Grandma Laura. I used her real first name to honor her and because she has been dead since 1966. I’ve created different names for some characters, while for others I used their actual first names with fictitious last names to protect the privacy of their remaining relatives.

After Grandma Laura died on Valentine’s Day~~,~~ in 1966, one month before my wedding, I learned a lot about her from my mother, June. I had known she was one-half Cherokee, but not that her full-blood

Cherokee mother had died when Laura was only three-years-old. For some unknown reason, Laura's father despised Indians, as Native Americans were called then, and forbid his children to admit to their Indian blood after their mother's death. He insisted they tell people they were "Black Irish" instead. That information stunned me. I considered Laura's Cherokee heritage an interesting and very special part of our family history, but never dreamed that she'd been taught to be ashamed of who she was. What must it have been like to live in fear that people would discover you were a "half-breed" that should be shunned or looked down upon?

My mom told me that Laura had run away from home as a young girl because her brother raped her. That part of her story was a little murky though, because mom wasn't positive if it was Laura's brother or her father, since they had the same name. That was my first executive decision writing the series—I made the rapist her father, but with the brother as a catalyst. Laura was the one who ran away in shame, though, since families didn't air their "dirty laundry" in public and fathers were the undisputed head of their households. Domestic violence wasn't a crime, just a "private family matter" that folks might gossip about, but never expected the local law to interfere with. Laura was convinced there was something wrong with her that caused her to be attacked—after all, no male relative would rape a girl unless she was provoking or inviting him, right?

Stories about Grandma Laura's psychic visions were part of family lore when I grew up. The one that haunted me the most took place when my mom was a young girl. The family rented a farm with a large house that had a living room big enough for dances on the weekends. My mom remembers how her parents pushed the furniture against the walls to create space for dancing, then played music and sang for hours for their guests.

No music this night, though, as a blizzard roared around the house depositing deep snowdrifts against the walls. Neither Laura nor the children could sleep. Their father wasn't there, since he'd been committed in a mental hospital for months after a complete mental breakdown. Mom doesn't remember the cause of the breakdown, so I created a story related to a horrible event in World War I.

June and Raymond, who was two years younger than his sister, took turns on a swing Laura had hung from the rafters. They took turns holding their baby brother David on their laps to keep him entertained. Laura stayed by her middle son's bedside, bathing Jimmy's body with cool cloths, trying to bring down a high fever. No doctor had seen him because of the horrible weather and Laura's inability to pay for a doctor's visit, and she feared her son might not make it through the night.

My mom remembers the shocked look on her mother's face when they heard a knock on the front door, the sound loud enough to carry above the raging storm. June planted her feet against the floor to stop the swing, her attention focused on her mother. Laura opened the door, then screamed and fainted. Her body slid down the door, pushing it shut, then lay still on the icy floor.

June and Raymond ran to Laura's side, locked the door, then patted their mom's face and arms, calling to her until she woke up. As soon as Laura opened her eyes, she bolted to Jimmy's side, tears pouring down her face, as she scooped him up into her arms. She held him for the rest of the night, releasing him only when his fever broke just before sunrise.

June learned months later that when Laura opened the door that stormy night, she saw a young man dressed in black. Not a single snowflake had settled on the man's clothing, and his feet hovered just above the snow-covered ground. His black cloak hung motionless around his body, in spite of the howling wind. The hood sheltered his head, but there was no face, just a blank area on the front of the skull. A black coffin stood upright behind him. The apparition didn't make a sound, but Laura believed the message meant Jimmy would die. Her interpretation was wrong because Jimmy lived, but Laura's favorite nephew died that night instead.

The account of what my mother remembered about that night—including the loud knock she and Raymond heard, as well as their mother's terrified response to what she saw outside the door—created a mental picture I can never forget.

Not all the stories Mom told me about Laura's visions were quite that dramatic. While Mom was pregnant with my youngest brother, Jerry, she was surprised to receive a beautiful, full-skirted, wool coat in the mail. She called her mother and said, "Mom, how in the world did you know I needed a coat?" Simple answer. Laura had a vision one night in which a hugely pregnant June visited her and said, "Mom, look at me. I'm so big my coat won't reach around my belly. And it's cold!"

While my mother and I have always been in awe of Grandma Laura's metaphysical gifts, the people around her when she was growing up were not. At that time, such gifts were called the "Second Sight" and considered either lies, fakery, or the work of the devil. Once again, Laura was told to hide a basic part of her nature from those around her.

When I learned these things about Laura's past, I couldn't help wondering how in the world someone could grow up and be a "normal person" after being taught to despise and feel shame about who she was. I loved my

Grandma Laura and appreciated all the nice things she'd done for me, but I felt guilty for not giving her the affection and attention she'd deserved. After writing my memoir and two books about animal rescue, I decided it was time to honor Laura and write about her life. Little did I know that her history was far more amazing than I'd ever dreamed, and she was much more courageous and determined than I could have imagined.

Before writing about Laura, I needed to learn all I could about her. My mother was the best source and enjoyed sharing her memories. The stories were disjointed, however, since my wonderful mom was in the early stages of dementia. She provided names of a few cousins and their children who filled in some additional blanks. From them I learned about Laura's mother's death when Laura was only three-years-old, and that the oldest daughter had to take over the mother's role at only twelve-years-old.

Very little is known about Laura's mom, in large part because of her early death. Her Cherokee heritage information has been passed down through the children and grandchildren, but tribal membership was never verified through the Dawes Act. I can only assume that, like many others at the time, her parents didn't trust the government and hid from the agents who forcibly enrolled Native Americans.

"The **Dawes Act**, commonly referred to as the **General Allotment Act** or **Dawes Severalty Act** of 1887, allowed the United States federal government to break up tribal ownership of reservation land and allocate parcels of land to individual Natives. Senator Henry Dawes of Massachusetts was the creator of the Dawes Act that passed under Grover Cleveland's presidency.

Like the vast majority of Americans, Senator Dawes believed in the cultural superiority of the Europeans who founded the United States. Believing the Anglo-Saxon heritage was the epitome of human civilization, the authors of the Dawes Act reasoned that if Natives were encouraged to: adopt western cultural ways, acquire private land ownership, and were individually responsible for their farm or ranch, they could then become assimilated into American society as productive citizens.

Captain Richard Pratt made the most explicit statement of this sentiment in a speech to the Annual Conference of Charities and Corrections in 1892. During Pratt's speech titled, '*Kill the Indian, Save the Man*,' he stated that Indian boarding schools were filled with children taken from their families, shipped hundreds of miles away from their homes, and are educated in American culture and values. Thus, completing the issue of a 'land in severalty' and, according to Pratt, releasing the Native

Americans from their Tribes, bringing them towards being U.S. citizens.

The purpose of the Dawes Act was to destroy Native cultures, create individual Americans, and open up land for white settlements on Native American reservation land.

Specifically, the Dawes Act provided:

- Land surveys of reservations
- Allotment of one-quarter section of land (160 acres) to each head of household
- Allotment of a one-eighth quarter to every person of the age 18 years or older
- Allotment of a one-eighth quarter to each organ under the age of 18 years
- Allotment of a one-sixteenth quarter to any other person under 18 years living or born before President Cleveland execute the Dawes Act
- The U.S. government could sell land not allotted to individual Native Americans to actual settlers.

Additionally, section six of the Dawes Act established that all individuals taking up allotments are subject to laws of the state or territory in which they reside. Furthermore, all Native Americans born within the United States that had taken up residence separate from any Native Tribe, and adopted the habits of civilized life ~~will~~ will be considered a U.S. citizen.

The policies of the United States government concerning Native nations changed several times from 1774 to 1871. Initially, treaties between the parties were signed to set borders and stipulate behaviors on both Native nations and the U.S. government; both parties were considered independent sovereign nations.

In 1831, Chief Justice John Marshall was the writer for the majority opinion for the case ***Cherokee Nation v. the State of Georgia***. Marshall described the Native American Tribes as 'dependent nations' and that the United States heavily resembled a guardian to the Native Tribes. Later in 1871, the **Indian Appropriations Act** was passed and is best described as simple war-making with Native Americans who were not located on reservations. The Dawes Act was a part of this policy transformation and only applied to Natives on the registers of the various reservations in the country; only these individuals would be eligible for land allotments under the Act.

Westward Expansion

As more and more immigrants from Europe entered the United States, they were encouraged by Congress to move west into the land of the Louisiana Purchase, increasing **westward expansion** through the laws of both the Indian Removal Act of 1830 and later, Homestead Act of 1862. The United States violated virtually every treaty signed by the U.S. as westward expansion continued.

Beginning in 1800 and onward, Americans were hungry for their land and, in many cases, for slaves to create large plantations on their land. Settlers quickly began immigrating to land that would later become the states of Alabama and Mississippi.

The Creek, Cherokee, Choctaw, and Chickasaw nations were the significant impediments to this westward expansion. In 1813, Major General Andrew Jackson led an expedition against the Creek nation, forcing the surrender of twenty million acres. These expeditions of white settler encroachment would soon become a pattern, repeating several times throughout the nineteenth century.

The continuing flood of white settlers into reduced Native territory led to the pass of the **Indian Removal Act of 1830** under Andrew Jackson's presidency by Congress on May 26. President Jackson signed the Act into law two days later.

Indian Removal Act

After Chief Justice Marshall's ruling describing Native Tribes as "dependent nations," the U.S. Court reversed itself about one year later. However, the United States continued to define Native American nations as wards of the U.S. government and not independent sovereign nations.

In 1830, President Jackson signed the **Indian Removal Act**, giving him the authority to relocate the "dependent nations" anywhere within the territorial limits of the United States. These limits included territory west of the Mississippi River, which had been recently gained through the **Louisiana Purchase**.

On December 6, 1830, Jackson addressed Congress with his message on "Indian Removal". He stated there were **two** significant impacts of the Removal Act:

1. By removing Natives from Mississippi and the western part of Alabama, those two states ~~can~~ can advance in population, wealth, and power.
2. To remove Natives and their uncivilized nature and become a civilized and Christian community.

The Native American resistance to the Indian Removal Act led Jackson to order military action in 1838, displacing sixteen thousand Cherokee to Indian Territory, currently known as Oklahoma. Close to four thousand Cherokee men, women, and children died during their displacement on the **Trail of Tears**.

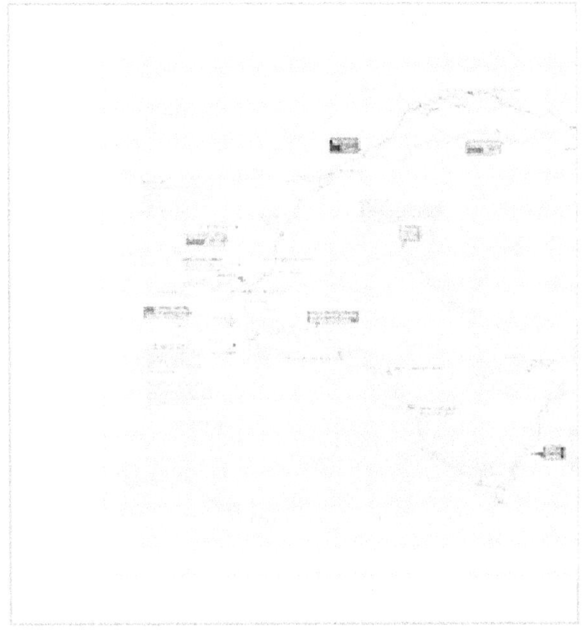

Map of Trail of Tears

Abolition of Treaty Making

After the **Fort Laramie Treaty** in 1868, which negotiated the defeat of the U.S. Army by combined forces of Lakota, Northern Cheyenne, and Arapaho nations, the United States government ceased making any treaties with Native American nations in 1871.

Only half of the treaties throughout the history of interactions between the United States and the various Native nations were ratified by Congress; none of the treaties were fully adhered to by the United States.

What Immediate Effects did the Dawes Act Have?

The Dawes Act reaffirmed the United States government's policy not to acknowledge Native nations as nations; instead, the government would relate to Native Americans only as individuals with no tribal affiliations. As a result of the Act, the United States stripped ninety million acres of land guaranteed through treaty to Native nations; the land was sold to non-native settlers. The Dawes Act destroyed the Native concept of communal ownership of land in favor of the western, capitalist notion that land is simply a commodity."

Ad for Indian Land lost after Dawes Act

INDIAN LAND FOR SALE

GET A HOME OF YOUR OWN

EASY PAYMENTS

PERFECT TITLE

POSSESSION WITHIN THIRTY DAYS

FINE LANDS IN THE WEST

IRRIGATED
IRRIGABLE

GRAZING

AGRICULTURAL
DRY FARMING

IN 1910 THE DEPARTMENT OF THE INTERIOR SOLD UNDER SEALED BIDS ALLOTTED INDIAN LAND AS FOLLOWS:

Location.	Acres.	Average Price per Acre.	Location.	Acres.	Average Price per Acre.
Colorado	5,211.21	$7.27	Oklahoma	34,664.00	$19.14
Idaho	17,013.00	24.85	Oregon	1,020.00	15.43
Kansas	1,684.50	33.45	South Dakota	120,445.00	16.53
Montana	11,034.00	9.86	Washington	4,879.00	41.37
Nebraska	5,641.00	36.65	Wisconsin	1,069.00	17.00
North Dakota	22,610.70	9.93	Wyoming	865.00	20.64

FOR THE YEAR 1911 IT IS ESTIMATED THAT **350,000** ACRES WILL BE OFFERED FOR SALE

For information as to the character of the land write for booklet, "INDIAN LANDS FOR SALE," to the Superintendent U. S. Indian School at any one of the following places:

WALTER L. FISHER, Secretary of the Interior

ROBERT G. VALENTINE, Commissioner of Indian Affairs

By all accounts, Laura's father, Jon, was a vicious, cruel man. During one of my critique group sessions while I was writing the first book, a male member of the group said, "I know this is based on a true story, but I cannot imagine any man being so brutal to his wife and children. What could have caused him to be that way?"

My answer was ridiculous. "I have no idea," I said. "I just know about the things he did." Then I realized that my job as a writer is to fill in those blanks so that readers could understand and accept the character of Laura's father, even if they hated his behavior. What a revelation! After a great deal of thought and research, I realized Jon was a creature of his time. He was born not that long after the end of the Civil War, when discrimination and cruelty went hand-in-hand. At that time, all women, no matter their color, were little more than chattel, with very few rights or protections. It was also a difficult economic time when daily survival for rural families was a challenge. I created Jon's back-story with all those things in mind so readers could accept him as a fully developed—albeit flawed and disagreeable—man.

As I tried to paint an accurate picture of Laura's father, one anecdote—which I did not put in the books—shared by my mom's cousin Shirley, stayed with me. Laura's only brother, Ben, was Shirley's father, and he ended up being almost as mean as his own dad. Jon, Laura's father, spent his last few years living with his son's family. He developed a type of cancer which resulted in horrible weeping wounds on his face, which his daughter-in-law cleaned and treated every day in spite of constant verbal abuse and humiliation. One day, when both parents were out of the house, Shirley remembers her disfigured grandpa calling the five children. She said they lined up in front of him, afraid of what he wanted, but not daring to disobey. He rubbed his hands over the oozing wounds on his face, then smeared that nasty fluid onto each child's delicate cheeks. Shirley told me that memory has haunted her for over ~~80~~ eighty years. She said Jon, her grandpa, died from the horrific facial cancer. When he passed on, the family didn't mourn, instead felt only relief at his passing.

Jon wasn't cruel to his first wife just because she was Indian—he also was furious at her for only producing one son during a time when sons were needed as labor on the farm and as heirs. After Laura's mother died, Jon remarried, choosing a young girl. She bore him two more daughters and was treated as cruelly as her predecessor.

The scant family memories, the timelines I found on ancestry.com for family births and deaths, plus family albums with pictures and notes, formed the skeletal framework for Laura's life story. Creating a book—I started out thinking it would be a single book—that conveyed the essence of this remarkable woman in relation to the times she lived in was the challenge. In order to meet it, I relied on my research assistant—Google—to help me fill in the specific details about places, history, and family life during the years Laura lived. My next challenge was to fill in all the blanks and create a story that flowed on a historical basis, while incorporating all the true events I'd learned about in a natural, believable way.

My best helper throughout the creation of the series was my grandmother herself. Before I fell asleep each night, I'd think about where the story had left off during my last session at the computer. Often during that hazy time between being fully awake and being asleep, the characters would appear in my mind, moving around and talking with one another. The same scenes, complete with dialogue and mental pictures of where they were and what they were doing, would play through several times until I drifted asleep. Then, when I sat down at my computer the next day, those scenes would pour through my fingers onto the keyboard, flying as fast as I could get them written. And once I got started, the pictures in my head would continue past the scenes from the ~~near-dream~~near dream state the night before and keep going forward. Sometimes I was quite surprised at the direction the characters took, especially if it was different from what I had planned. But if I tried to ignore them and proceed with the previous scenario I had created on my own, my mental pictures would ~~disappear~~disappear, and I couldn't create anything. I learned to trust the characters in my head and let them lead me. Chief among them was Laura, whose guiding hand directed me through the entire series.

Chapter Two

INDIAN TERRITORY NUMBER SIX

With only a basic story skeleton to work with, much of this series is rightly described as fiction because I had to create all the flesh to fill it out. Just in case there's a surviving relative out there who might take offense at how I developed the story framework and created personalities and lives for people I knew very little about, my apologies. Laura is the only one in the family whose real first name was used in book one, *She Survives.*

Laura was born and grew up in a sod house a few miles from Ardmore in what was then known as Indian Territory Number Six, which later became the state of Oklahoma. She was the fifth child after three sisters and a brother, with one sister born after her. Their mother died when Laura was only three years old, most likely, according to the surviving records, from Typhus.

I created the characters of ~~three of~~ Laura's three youngest sisters in the book, Lizbeth, Becca, and Bonnie, from my imagination, together with what I received from my dream vision's pictures. Their behavior, as well as their later lives, evolved under the careful guidance of the real Laura's dream help and the needs of the plot.

The character and story development of her brother, though, was a bit different. I knew from family stories that Laura's brother had grown into a detestable man, very much like his father. But little boys are not born destined to turn into monsters. How did it happen? And how painful was that process for his mother and sisters to watch as he changed? I wanted the growth of an innocent little boy into a mean, vicious man to be both believable and understandable to readers. I also wanted them to mourn for the changes the little guy went through simply because he wanted affection and approval from the father he loved and admired.

Ruth, the oldest sister, assumed the responsibilities of running the household and raising the children after the death of their mother. It was a huge burden for a twelve-year-old child, but not an unusual one for the times. She ceased being considered a young girl and became the woman of the house, as well as the de facto mother of her siblings. The incident in the book where her father beat her with a horsewhip is true. No one knows the actual reason for the attack, but the beating was so severe that both her dress and the skin on her back were shredded by the force of the vicious blows. The real Ruth ran away to get help from a neighbor, but returned home after her wounds healed.

Who was the neighbor who saved Ruth's life? That information has died with the family members, but it had to be someone who lived reasonably close by and who had some training in healing. Miz Dobbs was my answer. During the 1800s and early 1900s, most births took place at home, whether in a fancy mansion or a humble sod house, with the help of a midwife. Experienced midwives were highly prized and respected members of the community, who were expected to apply their knowledge of birth and healing to everything from births to injuries or diseases, and often extended their help for local animals as well. They frequently ended up assisting their neighbors with injuries and illnesses, even sometimes tending to their animals, making her the ideal choice.

Why did I change history and have Ruth run away instead of returning home? That was part of my solution to a major puzzle with Laura's story. I knew Ruth was horsewhipped to within an inch of her life by their father. I knew Laura was raped, ran away, and then ended up working as a cowgirl on a ranch. Girls and young women working as cowhands were rare during the early 1900s, even though a few female performers on horseback were featured in popular Wild West ~~Shows~~shows. The most famous of them all was Calamity Jane, born Martha Jane

Canary, the most well-known frontierswoman in her day, who joined Buffalo Bill's show as a storyteller. No one still living knows how or where Laura ended up with the unlikely job of working cattle from horseback, but my job as a writer was to invent a story where those true events could happen in a natural, believable sequence.

First step, I needed a neighbor to save poor Ruth, and Miz Dobbs seemed the most likely candidate. In addition to assisting with births, midwives also accumulated intimate knowledge of the townspeople they served. Miz Dobbs' actions and conversations with Laura's family during birthings, and after Ruth's beating, would be in accordance with practices of the time.

And then came the character of Emma, the owner of the ranch where Laura lived after she escaped from her father. Somehow, I had to create a pathway for Laura to end up with Emma where she could work as a real-life cowgirl. Step one was when Ruth left home after she was beaten and took refuge with the Carpenter family, where she fell in love and eventually married their son, Paul. The Carpenters needed to be people of some means to satisfy the plot requirements, so I made them the owners of the general store in Ardmore, Oklahoma. Laura's exploration of the store when she visited it with Ruth as an eight-year-old child also provided the perfect vehicle for readers to learn more about the times through the goods that Laura saw and her reaction to them.

The Carpenters sheltered Ruth after she escaped her father. When Laura turned up in the middle of the night after being raped, they wanted to save her as well, but because she was a minor, she would have been sent back to her father by the local sheriff. The perfect solution was for her to go to Mrs. Carpenter's sister, Emma. Laura's escape worked, and the plot now provided the perfect opportunity for the next events that happened in the real Laura's life.

Since the Carpenters became Ruth's in-laws and lifesavers for both Ruth and Laura, they are vital characters in the series. They are also my creations. None of the spouses and children of Laura's siblings were modeled after the real ~~ones, since~~ones since I have no information about them. If there is any resemblance, it comes from the source of my dream movies.

Laura and her sister, Lizbeth

Chapter Three

LAURA LEARNED TO CARE ABOUT NEWS

I've had numerous readers tell me that Emma is their favorite character. They love her courage, her fierce independence, and her intelligence. They also admire her for insisting she could do anything a man could do, and then doing it. She's hard-driven and determined, but also soft-hearted and compassionate for those in need. Emma is one of my favorite people in *She Survives,* too—and one I'm very proud to have created. She serves several important functions in the story. She is the one who provided a safe place for Laura to land when she had to run away and is the owner of a working ranch where Laura could fulfill her cowgirl duties.

Emma's ranch paints a picture of life at a different social and economic level than what Laura knew growing up in a sod house. Life for Laura during her years with Emma expanded her education beyond what she got in school, while nurturing her love of learning. For the first time, Laura learned to care about news beyond her immediate circle.

One of Laura's greatest passions throughout her life was a deep love of music. I remember her singing while she played the piano, accordion, violin, and banjo. My brothers and I rolled our eyes at the less than tuneful performances, but couldn't help smiling at her infectious enthusiasm. Years later, when I learned that her discordant playing and singing resulted from her hearing loss because of multiple untreated ear infections, I felt deeply ashamed of our lack of understanding and sympathy. It hurt to know that her love for her children and determination to keep them fed and healthy caused her to neglect herself and lose something so precious as a result. Laura's passionate love of music needed to shine through in these books, and Emma helped make that possible.

The awful rape that precipitated Laura's escape to Emma's ranch was real, although the actual scene itself had to be fictionalized. It had to be included because of the impact on her entire life. Talking about it was forbidden, first by her father and then because people didn't "air their dirty linen" in public. Unpleasant or private things were simply not revealed in front of people outside of the family. Fear of retribution and shame, caused by the belief that she was to blame for being raped, kept Laura silent about what had happened, but no doubt left internal scars.

The rape and accidental killing of Laura's youngest sister by their brother was not based on fact. I was told that the real Bonnie had some undiagnosed mental issues, but she lived into adulthood. Why, then, would I want to invent such a horrific act? The entire scene was enacted during one of my pre-sleep visions. It was powerful and terrible, but the perfect vehicle to portray what Ben had become in his emulation of their father. And since it was revealed in the story as a vision that Laura shared with Ruth, it demonstrated the clarity and intensity of her "second sight." Ruth was forced to acknowledge the truth of the vision, but immediately warned Laura of the dangerous potential consequences of ever sharing her gifts with other people.

Book Two,

Strive and Protect

Chapter Four

GLEN'S MENTAL BREAKDOWN

Creating Book Two, *Strive and Protect*, presented unique problems. The climax was Glen's mental breakdown, but a huge amount of time and multiple true events needed to be covered before that happened.

-At the beginning of the book, Laura had to be living in the closest large city to Emma's ranch, with her own place and a job. She had to fall in love with a rich, handsome man who swept her off her feet and then broke her heart. Then Laura needed to find work in a hospital. Because of the disastrous ending of her first love, Laura didn't believe in or trust romantic love, but still wanted a family, so she accepted the first proposal she received. My mother, Laura's first child in the book, was born in Seminole, Oklahoma. Laura and her husband lived with a relative for several years, then left because of the woman's cruelty toward June.

-The family ended up on the road during the Great Depression, with Glen doing odd jobs to keep them alive. He finally started work with the WPA (Works Progress Administration) handling heavy machinery. The family lived under a bridge one summer when June was five. They lived on a farm that everyone loved and where David was born. And then came Glen's breakdown.

The series of actual events that had to be included—listed above—was a long one, but I also needed to cover less tangible elements of Laura's identity. Instances of Laura's "second sight" had to be incorporated into the book to show how it worked for her and how her gifts grew. Music was also essential to Laura, so I needed to write about both her love for music and the growth of her musical talent. Even though this series has four separate books, each has to stand on its own for those readers who start in the middle. That meant I had to review Laura's family history and bring readers up to date on the status of each family member without too much repetition for those readers who had read the first book.

People don't live in a vacuum, so the history of the time also has to live for readers. The Great Depression was an incredible part of our country's history and Laura's life. The fear of another war breaking out was terrifying, and that needed to be real for readers, too.

My task for *Strive and Protect* was to include all of the above in a natural, smooth flow so that each event seemed spontaneous. Now you know why the book is so long, and focused on people and passing time, rather than Laura's inner emotions.

Strive and Protect begins in Tulsa, Oklahoma, for a couple of reasons. It was the closest major city to Emma's ranch and had thriving hospitals. We rejoin her story when Laura was twenty, and learn that she has been in the city for two years. She lives at the YWCA (Young Women's Christian Association), where she felt safe, and supported herself doing clerical work at an insurance company.

For the first time in her life, Laura has a boyfriend, Bruce Erickson, who was rich and handsome, just like the boyfriend who broke the real Laura's heart. The circumstances in the book match what actually happened, but all the personal details—Bruce's banker father, the luxury car, his parent's plans for his future, and the courtship details—were invented. Dialogue between Laura and Bruce offered the perfect opportunity for her to share details about her emotions and family history, including the horrible incident when she'd been raped by her father. The conversations also showed how safe Laura felt with Bruce. She loved him and believed he loved her as well, and felt utterly ~~betrayed at~~betrayed at Bruce's proposal for a weekend trip. The whole scenario confirmed her belief that something had to be wrong with her that caused men to think she would welcome inappropriate attention and behavior.

Laura all dressed up, pretty but proper.

After Laura slapped Bruce, she feared he would have her arrested. ~~So~~So, she took her money out of his father's bank, traveled to a hospital on the other side of town, and applied for a housekeeping job, then found new lodgings in a hotel for young women. She didn't tell anyone from the YWCA or her old job where she'd gone. ~~Lots~~ A lot of incidental characters join the lineup after her move—the women who lived at Thompson's Hotel, the hospital staff, and the patients. Laura's interaction with Phillip Dunn, who the doctors didn't expect to survive, is poignant and heart-rending, but had no basis in reality per my knowledge.

What I did know was that Laura ran from Bruce and ended up working in a hospital. She was so disillusioned that she vowed to never risk being hurt by falling in love again. I also knew that Laura spent many years working in hospitals and have no doubt that her intuitive gifts made a difference in her understanding of and ability to comfort her patients.

Laura hadn't seen her sisters in years and missed them terribly, but didn't have enough money to even think of traveling to visit them. Since it was important to the story for her to go there, I had her oldest sister, Ruth, pay for the train tickets.

One of the biggest challenges of writing a series is the need to introduce readers to the cast of characters. Even if they've finished the previous books, the writer needs to catch them up without boring them, while skimming all the vital history for new readers. The trip to Ardmore, Oklahoma accomplishes that goal, and more.

-Two of Laura's sisters are married and have children. Laura had known that Lizbeth, her second oldest sister, had married a much older widower with several children in order to escape the family home. When Laura reached Ardmore, she was surprised and happy to learn that Lizbeth and her husband had fallen in love and had a beautiful baby girl of their own. Of course, the family members I described in the book are fictional. If any of them resemble the real husbands or children, it's pure luck attributable to the guidance of my dream movies. They came to me fully fleshed out, with unique characteristics and personal stories, from the nightly visions I had during the writing of the series. The reunion with her sisters increased Laura's determination to have a happy family of her own someday, and showed her that even if she wasn't in love with her husband, it was possible.

Laura's Pa also lived in Ardmore, and in the ~~book~~book, she ends up face to face with him in the middle of town. Again, this is a fictitious event, but including it was important to show her growth into a strong, courageous woman no longer willing to be bullied by her vicious father.

Chapter Five

SHE WASN'T IN LOVE WITH HIM

Glen, Laura's future husband, was my real grandfather, but we know nothing about his history before they met.

Glen, unknown age or location

We do know that he loved music as much as Laura did and that it was the glue that held their friendship together. He was a good man and a good friend, so when he proposed, Laura accepted, even though she wasn't in love with him. She thought she was through with romantic love after Bruce hurt her, but wanted a family and children more than anything.

Laura and Glen's wedding picture. She was 22 and he was 23.

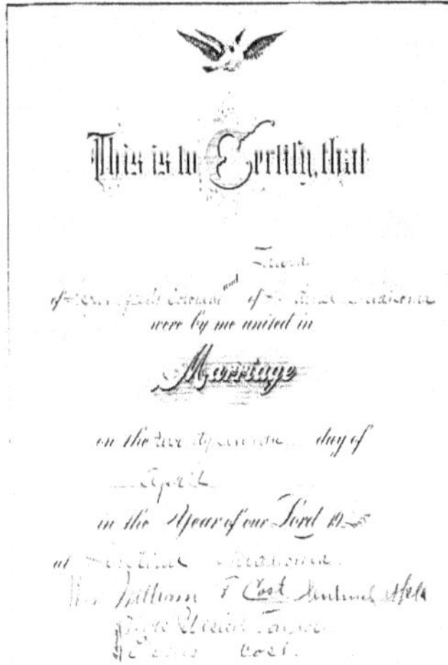

This is to Certify, that

Laura

of [illegible] and of [illegible]

were by me united in

Marriage

on the [illegible] day of

April

in the Year of our Lord 19[illegible]

at [illegible]

[illegible]

Laura and Glen's marriage certificate. The names are blocked out since only Laura's first name was used in the book.

Once Laura was married, I had to figure out why in the world they moved to Seminole, Oklahoma, where my mother was born. I had been told that my mother was Laura’s first child, but learned from a notation on an old photo that Laura gave birth to two baby girls before Mom was born. Those babies only lived a short time. I learned about them while finishing the last book, much too late to include in the story.

I went b~~B~~ack to Google to research what was going in Seminole between 1925 and 1926. The answer was an oil boom, with caused a huge population growth. Seminole, named for what was the smallest and poorest of the "Five Civilized Tribes"—Cherokee, Chickasaw, Choctaw, Creek and Seminole—in Oklahoma, went from a poor farming community in the early 1920s to a city that produced 2.6% of the world's oil production. The population exploded from 23,808 in 1920 to 79,621 in 1930. Perfect excuse for a man with mechanical skills and a desire to build a future to move from Tulsa to Seminole.

Glen and Laura's road trip to Seminole is half factual and half fictional. Laura's husband- did have a box truck that he modified by adding windows to make it more livable. The road conditions described as they traveled, as well as the names of all the little cities between Tulsa and Seminole, are based on maps of the time. All the day-to-day descriptions of their lodgings and Glen's work are fictional, but based on research and also on what we know about his skill with large machinery.

Seminole's primary importance to the story is because June, my future mother, was born there.

That fact was the perfect opportunity for me to create one of my favorite characters. Mouse was the half-black, half-Seminole midwife who delivered June. She was the ideal vehicle to bring in not only some information about the history and mistreatment of the Seminole

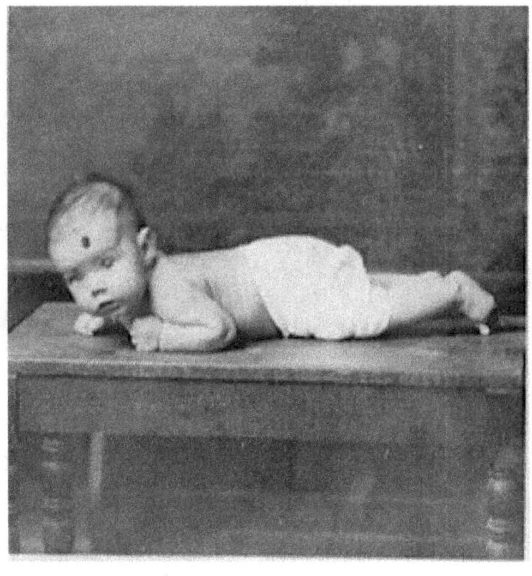

June, my mother, as a three-month-old above, and as a toddler next page. The mark on baby June's forehead is a mar on the old photograph.

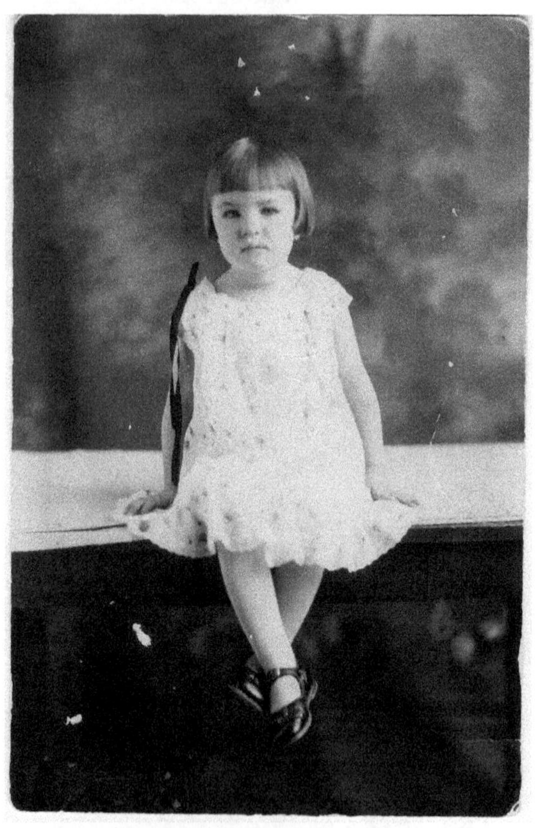

people in Oklahoma, but also the fact that members of the "Five Civilized Tribes"—so named because they were considered more assimilated into white culture than other tribes—purchased and kept ~~black~~ Black slaves just like the white people they emulated. Unfortunately, both the Seminoles and ~~black~~

Black people were discriminated against and mistreated by the white population.

Mouse shared the same psychic gifts as Laura, except that she saw spirits as well as ~~hearing~~ heard them. Laura was astonished when Mouse told her she'd been visited by Laura's mother. And as a result of that visit, Mouse knew all about Laura and when to expect her, which enhanced Laura's trust in Mouse and in her own spiritual gifts. The best description of Mouse's gifts and beliefs is Shamanism, which was and still is a vital belief system practiced in virtually every indigenous culture across the planet. It is a practice rooted in the presence, gratitude, and inter-connectivity of all things. This spiritual belief isn't actually a religion, but coexists with other religions and cultures who believe in spirits and that they communicate with people.

The explosive growth of the city of Seminole declined almost as fast when the enormous production volume glutted oil markets, causing a price collapse that resulted in the oilfields being placed under state control.

The next known bit of history about Laura was her move away from Seminole to South Dakota, where the little family lived with one of her husband's relatives. No one knows why they moved away from Seminole, or if they did so before or after the oil crash, but it was a perfect opportunity for me to describe one possible scenario based on Laura's second sight. The warning from Laura's mother saved the family from potential financial ruin and illustrated the problem Glen had dealing with Laura's psychic gifts. He didn't want to put any credence in information that she said came from her dead mother. In an effort to convince him, Laura told Glen about what she had seen in his dreams—the deaths of both his brother and his mother. He agreed to leave Seminole because he couldn't deny the truth of what she told him, but was both shocked and shaken by her words.

The next conundrum was what relative of Glen's would take him and his family in. My mom told me she remembered going to Glen's parents' place, but she gave me that tidbit after I had already killed his parents off in the books. I didn't want to do a massive rewrite, so his real-life parents changed into an uncle and aunt. The true mistreatment of the children was by their grandmother, Glen's mother. Mom remembers the final straw before they moved away was when the tips of her fingers were caught and crushed in an old-fashioned washing machine wringer. Her grandmother didn't hit the switch to open the wringer until June's fingers were sucked in up to her hand. The wringer broke one finger, but the woman had no compassion, just an admonition for June to be more careful next time.

I have no idea why a woman would be so mean to her own grandchildren, but I had to figure out a reason for the woman in the story, Glen's aunt, to turn on his children. My answer was to borrow and modify a real tragedy as the catalyst. As an adult, Laura's brother lost two of his sons, a seven-year-old and a nine-year-old, who died when they either climbed or fell into an unlocked fuel tank on the family farm. I can't imagine the pain and guilt their father must have felt for not padlocking the lid of the tank to keep the children out. Since I'm not knowledgeable about fuel tanks, I changed the fuel tank into a cistern, which would be a very common item on a farm.

Children Die in Fuel Tank

This newspaper picture shows Ben, Laura's brother, as an adult, standing next to the fuel tank where two of his sons died. The little boys would have died very quickly from the fumes, even if they had been able to swim.

Many farms had such tanks for fuel to run their tractors and trucks. The round lid has a ring at the base for a padlock. The spigot coming out of the top was used to dispense gas out of the tank.

In *Strive and Protect,* Dennis and Gladys, Glen's uncle and aunt, lost both their twin boys to drowning in a cistern many years prior to their appearance in the story. The painful loss drove Gladys to seek comfort in a bitter and rigid Christian faith that leached all the love, joy, and tenderness out of her. It took several years for her enmity toward Laura and the loving way she parented her children to develop and grow. During those years, Raymond and Jimmy were born with only sullen Gladys at Laura's side. The tipping point was an incident where Gladys beat the two oldest children, only five and two at the time, with a tree branch. When that happened, Laura insisted to Glen that the family must leave, even if it meant joining thousands of other homeless people living on the road.

Like most parents during the Great Depression, Laura depended on inexpensive patent medicines to treat the family. When the children were beaten by Gladys, Laura treated the welts with Cloverine Salve, then gave them Konjola Syrup to calm them and help them sleep. Both of those real products were extremely popular.

Cloverine Salve was patented in 1894 and first produced in 1895. The ingredients were a blend of white petrolatum, turpentine oil, white wax, and perfume. The directions were to

The Cloverine Salve tin container kept the same design for many years, changing only the price.

"Apply freely, and repeat as often as needed for temporary relief of minor irritations of the skin." The product promised to remove wrinkles, heal cuts and burns, and give your skin a glowing complexion.

One of the most interesting things about Cloverine Salve was the method the company chose for selling it. George C. "Bud" Wilson, son of the company owner, got the idea of running an ad in the Famous Funnies comic books offering premium prizes to young boys willing to sell the salve "door to door." The idea was brilliant—at one time 300,000 young salesmen were knocking on doors selling Cloverine Salve.

1931 magazine ad for Cloverine Salve salesmen.

The Konjola Syrup Laura used was created and marketed by one of the most interesting characters of the Roaring Twenties, Gilbert Mosby, the "Konjola King." The exact ingredients of the medication were never revealed, but Mosby claimed that Konjola would cure nervousness, indigestion, rheumatism, neuritis, catarrh (excessive discharge or buildup of mucus in the nose or throat, associated with inflammation of the mucous membrane), constipation, stomach trouble, general weakness, kidney problems, and liver dysfunction. It was known to contain a lot of herbs, as well as the secret to Mosby's success in the Prohibition era—a liberal portion of alcohol.

Konjola Syrup bottle with Gilbert Mosby's face etched in the glass.

I exercised a bit of "poetic license" in describing Laura's use of the syrup since Gilbert's company went under in 1934. But I imagine that ~~lots~~ a lot of the product was still in the supply chain and people's homes since it was considered a cure for so many common medical problems.

Chapter Six

THE GREAT DEPRESSION

Like everyone else, I knew about the Great Depression. That is, I knew it started with the stock market crash in 1929 and didn't end until the start of World War II. But knowing statistics such as unemployment going from 3% in 1929 to 25% in 1933, that the average family income dropped 40% while more than $1 billion in bank deposits were lost due to bank closings, and that hundreds of thousands of families lost their homes to foreclosure is only a fraction of the story.

-We tend to forget that severe drought hit the Midwest and Southern Great Plains in 1930, causing massive dust storms beginning in 1931. The effects of the Dust Bowl on top of the Great Depression caused a huge migration away from the worst hit areas, with over 300,000 people moving to California. One of the best accounts of the economic collapse and migration to the West is John Steinbeck's epic *The Grapes of Wrath*.

Life in South Dakota for Laura's family was at the mercy of both the economic crisis and the awful dust storms. And when they left the farm, humble and miserable though it was, things were even more difficult on the road. None of my family's stories about daily life back then have survived. June, my mom, is the only survivor from her immediate family, and only remembers that they lived in the truck that her daddy had fixed up for them. It was packed with all of their possessions and whatever provisions they had at any given time. I have to give great credit to both Laura and Glen for doing such an amazing job of sheltering their children from the harsh realities of their life on the road.

Strive and Protect contains several stories about encounters Glen and Laura had with people on the road. Some needed help and were happy to share their own provisions in trade for Glen's labor. Others were suspicious and paranoid about anyone who approached them. My purpose in creating those stories was to illustrate what life was like for people, like Laura's family, who were homeless and looking for work to sustain themselves. The stories also are there to show how desperate life was for those who stayed on their land and tried to eke out a living in spite of what appeared to be insurmountable odds. The most heartbreaking of these stories was when Glen and Laura drove up to a farmhouse where the bodies of the people were in the barn, dead from a murder suicide. Each of the stories came to me at night, during my visions before I fell asleep. I believe that Laura sent them to me and that they were a good reflection of what life was like during those awful times.

Surviving the Great Depression was not easy, and most people blamed President Hoover for their suffering. Their anger—as well as a dry sense of humor—was reflected in what are called "Hooverisms" or names for everyday items. Some of the most common were Hoover heaters for campfires, Hoover houses for cardboard boxes, Hoover blankets for newspapers, Hoover shoes for worn-out footwear, Hoover hogs for wild rabbits or armadillos killed for food, and Hoover stew for food served in soup kitchens. An unusual fact I unearthed while researching Hooverisms was that one of the largest soup kitchens in Chicago served Thanksgiving dinner to ~~5,000~~five thousand Chicagoans in 1930. That soup kitchen was owned and managed by Al Capone.

Only three Hooverisms appear in *Strive and Protect*. The first is when Laura is watching a woman flirt with three men outside of a bar, while Glen has gone to see about potential jobs. ~~They responded~~They responded to her by pulling their front pants pockets inside out. The pockets, looking like limp rabbit ears, were called Hoover flags and meant that the men had no money—nothing at all. Their Hoover flags did not impress the fancy young lady, who turned away and stomped back into the bar.

Laura and Glen met a very important family on the road. Isaac and Willa York, together with their son Ruben, were stuck by the side of the road by a shredded tire. Glen stopped to see if he could help, and the two couples struck up an instant friendship that lasted throughout their lives. The Yorks were traveling in a Hoover wagon, a broken-down car pulled by a draft horse. A lot of people had cars during the Great Depression, but the cost of maintenance and gas forced many to resort back to the power of a horse or mule to propel the car.

Unlike the one pictured above, the York's Hoover wagon was packed inside and out with all of their possessions as well as provisions for them and for the big draft horse that pulled it.

The introduction of the Yorks provided a picture of a different class of Americans and of how the Great Depression affected them. Isaac was well educated and had been a bank manager in Sioux City. But when his bank failed, he lost his job, then they lost their money and their home. Glen changed his plan to go to Sioux City, Iowa and look for work after Isaac explained that the huge Hooverville outside of the city was growing daily. Even with his advanced degrees and previously highly prized management skills, he hadn't been able to get a new job. Isaac gave Glen useful information about some New Deal jobs opening up with the WPA, but said that he and Willa were headed to California. Their decision in the book was because they had a doctor friend who lived in California. The doctor offered help for the York family to relocate, and also offered to help a very pregnant Willa deliver their baby.

All of those are good reasons for the creation of the York family in the story, but they were even more important for another reason. I knew that Laura would go to California later in the series, and I needed someone living there to help her. That someone had to be a close female friend she trusted and could confide in. Willa was the perfect answer.

Book Three,

Desperate Choices

Chapter Seven

ATTITUDES TOWARD MENTAL ILLNESS HAVEN'T EVOLVED MUCH

In the decades since Glen's collapse, public attitudes toward mental illness haven't evolved as much as we'd like to claim. There are more labels for individual mental illnesses now, as well as more medications and types of therapy available. But underneath those bright and shiny advances, mental illness is still often viewed as proof of a weak mind and something to be ashamed of and shunned. Unfortunately, the person suffering is all too often seen as a failure and avoided as if the condition was contagious.

-We still don't have treatments that are consistently successful for P.T.S.D. sufferers, and when Glen broke down in the 1930s, there were few treatment options for mental illnesses, and very limited successes. A few drugs, water therapy, electroshock treatments, and lobotomies for the most difficult cases were the only things available. No one knows what treatments my grandfather actually received, so I described those that were most likely to have been used on him—drugs, water treatments, and electroshock therapy.

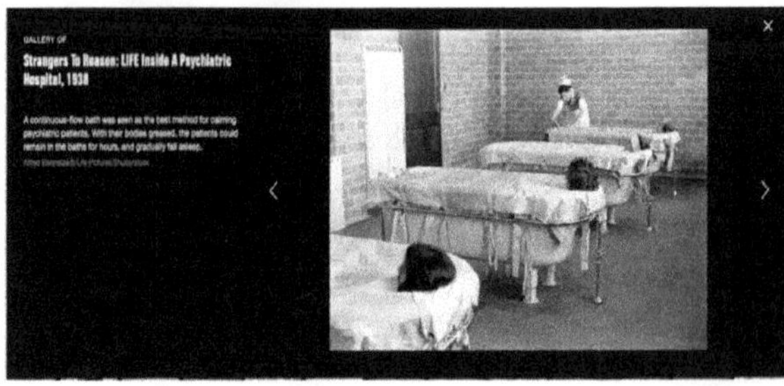

Laura's visits to the hospital had to have been painful, but I based them on research into the mental hospitals of the time, my imagination, and what I saw in my nightly visions. They were critical to show the conditions of the patients as well as the heartache of the family when faced with the reality of Glen's suffering. I also wanted to show the children's reactions, especially when they refused to go visit their father at the hospital after the first time.

-Attitudes toward mental illness, especially for someone incarcerated in a mental institution, were harsh. Children are cruel anyway, and tend to innocently repeat comments their parents make with no thought about how hurtful their words might be. There are no secrets in small towns, so I'm sure the schoolmates would have made life difficult for Laura's children with remarks about their crazy father stuck in a nuthouse. They had to survive in school, so withdrawing from their father made total sense.

Having Glen hospitalized also illustrated another issue for Laura and women of her day. Gender roles were rigid, with the man of the family expected to provide for his wife and children. With few exceptions, men handled the finances so the wives could concentrate on taking care of the household and children. Suddenly alone, Laura realized she had to pay the bills with what little they had, but was shocked to discover that her name wasn't on their checking account. I don't know if that actually happened, but it made sense to put her in that situation. How embarrassing it would have been to have to beg the bank officer and then Glen's doctor for help in order to access the family money.

There is no known explanation for why the real Glen suddenly returned to reality after four months in the hospital. We do know he panicked when he realized his wife and four young children were all alone with no one to provide for them. He was desperate to get out of the hospital and return home, but was not permitted to leave. I wrote fictional scenes and dialogue about his efforts, but the reawakening and escape really happened and the outcome described in the book was true.

Glen attacked a guard, causing serious injuries, and escaped, only to be chased down by dogs and savagely beaten with chains by the men who caught him. He suffered severe brain damage from the chain wounds, and carried scars on his head and upper back for the rest of his life. Nothing was done to Glen's captors, but after he was ~~apprehended~~apprehended, he was transferred to an institution for the criminally insane because he hurt a man during his escape.

Several readers have asked me to reassure them that Glen recovers and returns to his family. I would have loved to write that heartwarming scene, but ~~unfortunately~~unfortunately, he spent nearly the rest of his life institutionalized, leaving Laura to raise their children alone.

Pacing in writing is important, so I made sure to include ~~lots~~ a lot of family interactions between Laura and the children to lighten the mood and portray the love between them. One of my favorite scenes is about the beans and the pressure cooker, but it didn't happen in the way it appears in the book. In fact, it didn't happen to Laura at all, but seemed perfect to include. The great bean explosion—and those beans and juice shot out of the tiny opening at the top of the cooker like bullets from a machine gun—happened when I was a little girl. The only difference is that I don't remember any laughter breaking out as the beans and juice ran down the walls and dripped from the ceiling. My memory is of shock, and then indignant anger when I was drafted into working with my mom to clean up the incredible mess.

Laura did all she could to make every penny stretch. My mom remembers only having two dresses for school. As soon as she got home from classes, she changed into stained play-clothes so Laura could wash her school dress in the sink and hang it to dry. In winter the dress would hang inside the house so it would be dry and ironed to be worn every other day. June was called ugly nicknames by some of the girls from wealthier families for only having two school dresses. She begged her mom for more clothes, crying about how the girls constantly shamed her, but never appreciated the hard work of constant laundering, mending, and ironing.

Chapter Eight

THE COHEN FAMILY

The Cohen family, Harvey and Magda plus their daughter Helga, are three vital characters in the series. They are also often mentioned by readers as favorites—frequently with follow-up questions about what happened to them later. I am thrilled to know that people admire and relate to them, since I created them for very specific reasons related to the rise of Nazism in Germany and the resulting attitudes in the United States.

Harvey was an American Jewish soldier who met and married Magda after serving in Germany during and after the first World War. Magda's father, her only living relative, was a master furniture maker and a rabbi in the Pankow section of Berlin. He gave her permission to marry with one condition—Harvey had to promise not to take her away to America. The little family lived together after the marriage, and Harvey worked with his father-in-law in the furniture factory. They were overjoyed at Helga's birth and active in the various events and cultural offerings of the city until Hitler's fame and power began to rise.

Harvey begged Magda and her father to leave for America, fearing that even his American citizenship might not be enough to get his Jewish wife and daughter to safety. But the rabbi refused to leave his people, and Magda refused to leave her father. Then came the first night of Kristallnacht, November 9th, 1938, when German Nazis attacked Jewish people and their property. Magda's family hid in the basement, but her father tried to reason with the thugs and was beaten. When it was safe for them to venture out, Magda and Harvey found him dying on the floor. With his last words, he begged them to survive, so the little family escaped that very night. Yes, the story is fiction, but is based on experiences shared by many people who were lucky enough to escape.

I created this family not only to bring in what was happening in the world with the rise of the Nazis, but to illustrate the narrow mindset of a lot of the American people as well. Harvey was an American Jew with a German wife and daughter, who were also Jews. Yet way too many people then—as now—are incredibly narrow in their thinking. The family was German, so many Americans considered them to be allied with the Nazis. They were also Jewish, but instead of being considered victims who were lucky to escape persecution, they were viewed with suspicion and ostracized rather than welcomed.

Magda and Helga become close friends of Laura and June. Their discussions and interactions provide the perfect vehicle for exploring the emotions and fears of both families, as well as several significant historical events. The atrocities of the two nights of Kristallnacht are discussed in the books: f. First when we learn about the death of Magda's father, then later in the fourth book, *Her Triumph*, when Magda shares a story about the second night. discussed in the books.

The next true event that is woven into the story is that of the ship M.S. St. Louis which sailed from Hamburg for Cuba carrying over nine hundred Jews trying to escape from Germany. In the story, Magda's cousin Solomon had paid for passage, but missed the ship. Magda, of course, didn't know that was a blessing in disguise.

MS St. Louis - picture of the day

A photographic highlight selected by the picture desk. The MS St. Louis, a German ocean liner carrying over 937 Jewish refugees, was denied entry to the United States on this day in 1939. It had already been turned away from Cuba and would later be refused entry to Canada. When the ship returned to Europe it had been at sea for over a month. The passengers were finally given refuge in various European countries, but it is estimated that approximately a quarter of the passengers died in concentration camps.

Go to page 2 icture of the day | Art and design | The Guardian 3/3/23, 7:42 PM

Karin Andreasson

Tue 4 Jun 2013 11.17 EDT

Refugees arrive in Antwerp on the MS St. Louis after more than a month at sea, on 17 June 1939
Illustration: Photograph: Three Lions/Getty Images

The passengers on the M.S. St. Louis had paid for their tickets and obtained Cuban visas, but were denied entry when they reached the island. The ship sailed to Miami, Florida, and then on to a port in Canada—but were again refused entry. In spite of the stories about what the Germans were doing to the Jews, neither the United States nor Canada wanted to accept any refugees, so the ship returned to Europe. Holland, France, Great Britain and Belgium each took about two hundred passengers, but the rest were returned to Germany where most ended up going to concentration camps to die. That story has always haunted me—and seems so relevant today with refugees throughout the world in dire straits.

***

Laura's relationship with Magda and her family was the one shining light that made their life in their horrible third floor apartment bearable. My mom remembers the family's move from a farm they loved to a tiny, dark and dank apartment. She also remembers the rats and the bugs. The rats made late night trips to the bathroom scary because the rodents foraged after dark. ~~They were~~They were big, aggressive, and fast. In spite of Laura's vigilance in searching out and plugging up the rat holes and setting traps, she could never get rid of them.

Today the same methods Laura used are still around. There are more sophisticated poisons and traps, but those can still be dangerous in the house with small children and family pets. Traps have to be carefully hidden or can do severe damage to a child's hand or foot. Rats are smart animals too and can quickly become trap-wise. Laura's method of plugging rat holes with steel wool and caulk would still work safely today, even though it's messy.

Mom also remembers that the apartment walls were covered with newspaper. In the book Laura's apartment walls were covered with blank wallpaper backing, which would have been very cheap. The scene in which David pulls some of the paper off and frees hundreds or thousands of bugs actually happened. Mom recalls the hole in the paper alive with bugs that poured down the wall and spread over David and the floor. They sealed the hole as fast as they could, but getting rid of the bugs in the walls was impossible. She said that she and her brothers could lean against any of the apartment walls and hear the soft sibilance of the insects moving under the paper.

Chapter Nine

THE ELDERLY PAID A HIGH PRICE

Phoebe Zimmerman, the nearly deaf elderly widow that lived in the second-floor apartment below Laura's family, was another important character that was created out of whole cloth. The Great Depression ravaged people all over the world, but the elderly paid an even higher price as families were torn apart in a desperate attempt at survival. Prior to the Great Depression, the elderly often lived with their family members ~~,~~and contributed by working in whatever way they could. But when the Great Depression struck, family members begged for help in caring for their elderly relatives. Title I of the 1935 Social Security Act created a program, called Old Age Assistance (OAA), which gave cash payments to poor elderly people, regardless of their work record. ~~-~~OAA provided for a federal match of the state's old-age assistance expenditures.

"OAA was fabricated out of the ~~28~~twenty-eight-state old-age assistance programs that had been put in place by the early 1930's. These programs varied quite a bit, but they were mostly brought into the new federal system as-is. Each state was allowed to set its own standards for determining eligibility and payments, with the federal government providing cash for a ~~50%~~ fifty-percent match of up to ~~$30~~thirty dollars a month in aid. The lack of federal control was deliberate. The legislation was written that way to get the support of states that wanted the federal government's assistance without too many strings attached. Only a few federal requirements were added:

The old-age assistance program had to be available throughout the state, not just in certain counties.

The ~~State~~ state had to provide at least some of the financing for the program. (In some states the existing old-age assistance programs were only funded at the local level).

Residency requirements could not be any longer than ~~5~~ five out of the last nine~~9~~ years, and the minimum age for receiving benefits could not be any older than age ~~65~~sixty-five.

The state had to create a single state agency to administer the plan, and also establish a system of administration and reporting to the federal government.

The program had to include an appeals process for people who believed they had unfairly been denied old-age assistance.

If the state or local governments collected money from the estate of any recipient of old-age assistance, half of that money had to be given to the federal government.

Payments to anyone living in a "public institution" were prohibited.

All the other provisions of the existing plans continued into the OAA program. This meant that in many states OAA was not available to elderly people who had families who "ought" to be supporting them, and that beneficiaries could be required to turn over everything that they owned before receiving any assistance, while other states had no such restrictions. In fact, the state restrictions were quite severe:

All but Arizona and Hawaii refused to make payments to older people who had children or relatives who could support them.

Most limited assistance to elderly people who were age ~~65~~ sixty-five or older, but quite a few set the limit even higher, at age ~~75~~seventy-five.

Most required that beneficiaries must have been citizens and residents of the state for ~~15~~ fifteen years;~~,~~ some had even longer residency requirements than that.

Many required that the beneficiary must transfer to the pension authority any property they possessed before any payment would be made.

Most had property and income caps to limit eligibility, generally a maximum of ~~$3,000~~ three thousand in property and ~~$300–$365~~three hundred to three hundred and sixty-five a year in income.

Most required that benefits would be denied to anyone who gave away property in order to qualify for public assistance.

Most required that a lien be placed on the estate of the beneficiary to be collected upon their death.

Most required that recipients be "deserving", and benefits were denied to anyone who deserted a spouse, failed to support their families, had committed any crime, or had been a tramp or beggar.

Benefits were denied to inmates of jails, prisons, infirmaries, and insane asylums;~~,~~ although, a few permitted the payment of assistance for inmates of a benevolent fraternal institution.

Most set a cap on monthly payments at ~~$30~~thirty dollars a month, although they actually paid about half of that or ~~$15~~fifteen dollars a month on average.

The restrictions were so severe, and the number of states that actually had launched their plans and committed funds to them was so limited, that even in 1935, in the depths of the Depression, there were less than

~~200,000~~two hundred thousand people covered under state old-age assistance plans. (Old Age Security Staff Report, 1934)"

Reviewing these facts about how elderly people lived during the Great Depression helps clarify Mrs. Zimmerman's plight and why her son and his wife were happy to find someone to look after her. And of course, Laura desperately needed the income. The fact that her children and Mrs. Zimmerman fell in love with each other was just a bonus that told a lot about the way Laura raised her kids. The pain they felt when she died seemed more profound than that shown by her own family. And the realization that Laura would have to ask Mrs. Zimmerman's cold daughter-in-law for assistance would have been bitter indeed.

Book Four,

Her Triumph

Chapter Ten

AURORA'S WOMEN'S AUXILIARY

The luxurious Hillside Hotel in Aurora was a fitting location for the Aurora's Women's Auxiliary to meet since it was the fanciest place in town. I created the description from pictures of top hotels of the ~~time, since~~time since Chloe Zimmerman wouldn't have considered any place of lesser status. The women members were all wives or relatives of the most important men in town and would have considered the best, most prestigious place as their due. Rupert, the concierge reflected that self-importance and viewed Laura as someone beneath the hotel's standards. Laura was undeterred though because her mission was too vital.

I don't know the place Laura met with the ladies' group, but my mom remembers being told about how Laura pleaded with them for help when they were her last hope. And Laura wasn't given any concrete help from the arrogant Chloe Zimmerman—just a command to come back the following Friday to see if any of the other ladies could help. It was a long week to wait, but at least Magda's support when she learned what Laura was facing helped. Magda and Harvey loved Laura and her children, but Laura knew that her friends had suffered enormous hardships and didn't want to take advantage of them. In addition, her early training against ever accepting charity made it hard for her to keep asking for help.

The friendship between Magda and Laura was mirrored by the closeness between their daughters. And just as Magda schooled Laura on the political and social changes in Germany, Helga, normally quite shy about her past, told June about all the awful things she had experienced there. The fictitious Cohen family was the perfect story addition to make the world situation live for the readers.

Laura's greatest source of strength and comfort was always the presence of her mother. Vera had died when Laura was only three but had stayed near and communicated with her daughter throughout Laura's life, giving wise advice and wrapping Laura in love each time she made her presence known.

Whenever times are toughest for Laura (and the rest of us), family emergencies pop up. I used my own three brothers as models for June's, and they always seemed to be getting hurt—always accidents, but also always at the most inopportune times. Jimmy breaking his arm and cutting his face in a fall seemed very natural and was shown to me in my dream visions the night before I wrote it. And running out of food after getting a bill from the doctor, piling on one problem after another just felt right, too.

Laura had to replace Jimmy's ruined shirt at the All-Faith Thrift Store. Jimmy and David went with her. Jimmy had lots of questions about Sister Mary, the nun who ran the store and who had become a good friend to Laura. This was the perfect opportunity for Laura to explain different religions to Jimmy and showed her acceptance of all faiths.

The week of waiting was like an eternity, but it was hard to stay calm on the way to the hotel to find out if someone from the women's group would help her. The only option Laura was given was unimaginable. The women claimed that they had the children's welfare as their highest priority, but said Laura would have to abandon her children to help them. The ladies insisted that if Laura refused, the Children's Services Bureau could take her children and rule her unfit. My mother remembers hearing about the help her mom was given, but provided no details about where she went when she left the children, other than that she went to California. June, my mom, fared better than her brothers under the Children's Bureau's care. To this day she still remembers how much she sneezed and how her arms and hands broke out in a horrible painful and itchy rash when she was forced to use pink

Dreft laundry soap to wash dishes. She was excited to move to a boarding school in the Ozarks, where she stayed until she left high school to elope—but never had to use Dreft again!

Raymond had a very hard time being separated from his mother. He was sent to Boys' Town, but since he wasn't a delinquent, he hated it and kept running away. Jimmy and David were placed together in~~to~~ an old men's home, where Jimmy had to protect his baby brother from some of the dirty old men. All three boys ended up at a ranch with a horrible couple who wanted them for the money they got for fostering and for the free farm labor. The couple was not really named Stinnett, but their treatment of the boys came from my mom's stories of what her brothers told her. All three boys were there for years and hated the place with a passion. The only story about the real couple, that ~~mom~~ Mom told me that wasn't in the book, was a nasty trick they pulled on Laura a couple of times. They'd give her permission to come see the boys, then when she arrived after walking over ten miles, would tell her the boys were out in the fields working and wouldn't come in for a few hours. She would wait until there was just enough time to walk home before it got dark, then leave without seeing her sons.

I was told that all the boys escaped, but not the details. The story about how Raymond left, and then Jimmy and David got away was a total fiction, but the approximate ages were about right, and all the information about the hobo culture of that time is straight from my chief assistant, Google, and what appeared in my nightly visions.

Laura's three sons, from left to right Raymond (18), David (12) and Jimmy (17)

"What was hobo culture?

They willingly work for pay or food. In fact, they travel around the country as workers, not only because they enjoy the freedom, but also to earn a stake to get them through the winter. Tramps, as defined by the hobos, are people who travel, but prefer not to work, and bums neither travel nor work.

When the Great Depression hit, jobs dried up and families lost their houses and farms. In desperation, many hard-working, able-bodied men left

home in search of any work they could get. Thousands upon thousands of predominantly young, white, single men hopped on board the hobo culture, riding the rails in search of odd jobs and seasonal work. Lest you think this group was just a bunch of lazy, free-loading, trouble-causing bums, let's look at the ins and outs of the Great Depression's hobo culture."

Hobos used the nation's railway system as their mode of transportation. Source: (vox.com)

"Hobo Jungles

Groups of hobos often set up makeshift camps near railways. Like independent communities, the hobo camps, or jungles as they were called, provided the men with a safe place to spend the night, take a bath, bandage wounds, wash out clothes, swap stories, sing songs, and share a meal. But mostly, the hobo jungles offered a sense of belonging and comradery. Hobos could bond over their shared situation and exchange information about jobs and the locations of other hobo jungles. It was the companionship that drew the hobos together."-

"By-

- **Steve Persall** *Former Times staffer*

Published -Aug. 20, 1997|Updated -Oct. 1, 2005

They were the forgotten survivors of the Great Depression; children forced by faulty economics and family problems to grow up too soon, searching for a better life at the other end of a railway going anywhere.

An estimated ~~250,000~~ two hundred and fifty thousand boys and girls hopped onto passing freight trains for destinations unknown in the 1930s. All that these young hobos typically owned were the ragged clothes on their backs, cardboard shoes, and moxie. Some found a better opportunity at the next stop on the line. Many others weren't as lucky.

Seven of these survivors share their reminiscences of growing up transient in *Riding the Rails*, a documentary film.

Riding the Rails has crisscrossed the continent, just as its subjects did, and earned high marks at ~~21~~ twenty-one film festivals, including the prestigious Sundance gathering in Utah.

The creation of the ~~72~~seventy-two-minute documentary has been another sort of remarkable journey.

Filmmakers Michael Uys (pronounced "ace") and Lexy Lovell were inspired by a 1934 book, *Boy and Girl Tramps in America*, written by Thomas Minehan of the University of Minnesota. That book, along with director William Wellman's 1933 drama *Wild Boys of the Road*, painted a bleakly inspirational image of children living hand-to-mouth alongside more experienced vagrants.

"We pretty much hit pay dirt with Modern Maturity magazine," Uys said. "We thought we'd be lucky to get 20 (responses). We ended up receiving 3,000 letters from people who rode the rails and whittled that down to the seven that you meet in the film."

Taking center stage among those survivors is Bob "Guitar Whitey" Symmonds, who, at age ~~72~~seventy-two, took the filmmakers along for one of the tag-along train rides that he still takes on occasion to see America. "He does it now for adrenaline," Uys said. "Then, it was a necessity."

No one now living knows exactly how or when my uncle, Raymond, made his way to California, but he became a fiercely independent man and hard worker. He farmed, worked as a mechanic, and did gigs as a musician as well. Raymond, oldest of the three brothers, was the quintessential family man. He and his first wife had eight kids. The story about the children finding a loaded gun in a stack of trash, and his daughter being shot in the head with it is absolutely true—and if Laura hadn't woken up knowing she and George had to get to Raymond's place, his daughter would have died. The marriage didn't survive with both parent's riddled with guilt, but everyone got through the experience.

Raymond on his farm in California

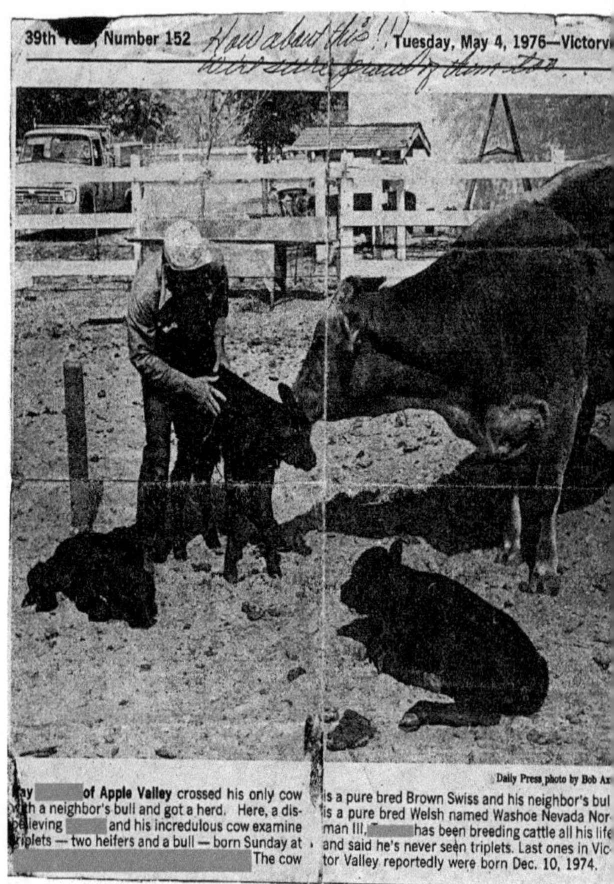

39th [illegible], Number 152 How about this!! Tuesday, May 4, 1976—Victorv

Daily Press photo by Bob Ax

ay of Apple Valley crossed his only cow with a neighbor's bull and got a herd. Here, a disbelieving and his incredulous cow examine triplets — two heifers and a bull — born Sunday at The cow is a pure bred Brown Swiss and his neighbor's bul is a pure bred Welsh named Washoe Nevada Norman III, has been breeding cattle all his life and said he's never seen triplets. Last ones in Victor Valley reportedly were born Dec. 10, 1974.

Ray's triplet calves in local newspaper.

Jimmy took a completely different path when he made his escape from the Stinnett ranch. Jimmy went into the Army and was sent to fight in Korea. The story Jimmy told his mom about the battle he fought was fictitious,[2] since I borrowed historical facts about the Battle of Bloody Ridge;[23] however, he was the only man left in his platoon and suffered tremendous survivor's guilt that finally sent him into a seminary to become a Baptist preacher and missionary. Jimmy, his wife Lela, and their four children lived most of their lives in Pakistan. Mere days after Jimmy and Lela's twentieth anniversary, he was killed. When his body was found in a ravine at the base of a nearby road where he had been jogging, the police assumed he'd been hit by a vehicle—later, after he was examined, they decided he had been beaten to death. No one was ever found responsible for his murder. Lela and the children returned to the United States, a place that did not feel like home to them.

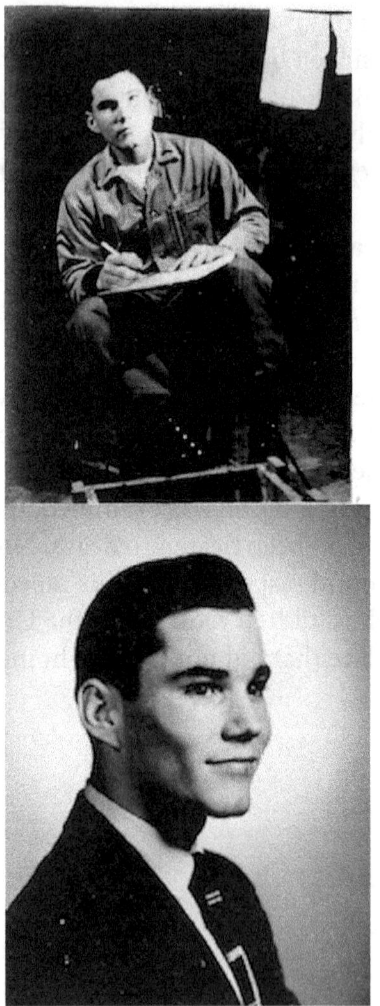

Jimmy in Korea

Reverend Jimmy

Sailor David and Pastor Jimmy

David, Baby-faced sailor

David also ended up in the military, serving in the Navy from when he was sixteen (back then it was easy to get away with lying about your age and everyone was trying to enlist after Pearl Harbor) until he retired at only thirty-six. He was one of the men who spent six months at the North Pole on the

U.S.S. Skate atomic submarine. His wife and five children always stayed on their farm in Missouri while David was deployed.

Family reunion in Hayward
Back row: Jack, June, Laura, George
June's kids in front:
Mike, Sharon (author) Jerry, and Patrick

The family reunion—the first time Laura and her children were all together after she was forced to leave them—really did take place at George and Laura's tiny house in Hayward. I remember that day, but as a little girl had no idea of the importance of the gathering.

Wrapping Up,

What Happened to

everybody?

Chapter Eleven

NOW YOU KNOW ALL THE SECRETS

Now you know all the secrets about the characters, the events, and the creative process for the Laura's Dash series. ~~s~~, so we can move on to events that took place to the real people that ~~wasn't~~ weren't revealed in the story.

-Laura's pa treated his second wife, Sarah, as cruelly as he did Vera, Laura's mom. Sarah bore him three additional daughters, but Ben, Laura's brother, was his only son. Jon blamed his wives for the lack of male children, and abused them and his daughters for the lack of the sons he wanted. He died at ~~66~~sixty-six, finally leaving his wife and daughters in peace. All of Laura's sisters married, had children, and lived normal lives for women of the times. They remained close to one another, geographically and emotionally, throughout their lives. Ruth, the oldest, remained the mother figure for the family ~~throughout her life~~. Ben, the only boy, unfortunately patterned himself after his father, becoming just as mean and cruel to his wife and children as his father had been.

Laura's husband, Glen, is probably the saddest character of all. He was a good man, but he proposed to Laura right after she was betrayed by Bruce, the banker. She accepted, but not because she loved him, rather because she wanted a family and considered Glen a good man and a good friend. So many readers have asked me to tell them that Glen's brain damage from the beating he suffered after escaping from the mental institution for the criminally insane was healed and he was able to return to his family. That never happened—instead he spent most of his life incarcerated, locked away from Laura and his children. June, Laura's daughter and my mother was able to get him out of the mental hospital system when Glen was in his 80s and brought him to her home in Sacramento to live. That arrangement didn't last too long, so he was moved into a memory care unit close to her home for a few short years. Diabetes ended up taking his life after multiple amputations from toes to his leg. He died in a hospital in Sacramento, with family around him, loved and well cared for at the end. Glen deserved more, but life seldom turns out as we'd script it.

Laura's sons grew into interesting men, very different from one another. -Raymond had a small ranch near Victorville, California, where his family raised cattle, but also was an excellent mechanic. In addition, he was a well-respected local musician, following in his parent's footsteps.

Jimmy, together with his wife and their four children, served as a Baptist missionary in Pakistan until his death. The assumption was that he was beaten to death by locals who resented his attempts to convert them from their own religions. Jimmy was a very strict Baptist (If it was fun but not in the Bible, it was probably forbidden). Lela and the kids restarted their lives as average Americans after his death.

David was a happy, successful man with a satisfying Navy career, followed by years working his farm with his wife and five children. He was truly a baby-faced sailor though. Three teenaged girls followed him to George's house from the train station, flirting and trying to get his phone number. They didn't believe that he was married and had children! He passed away, but left his family well provided for.

Now to bring you up to date on June, Laura's only daughter and my precious mother. June and Laura were close throughout June's life, best friends and confidants, sharing secrets and giggles. Their last conversation took place on Feb 13th, 1966, on the phone.

Laura had spent the day shopping for a dress for my wedding and found one she loved. Before calling June, she had called each of her sons and had long conversations with ~~each of~~ them. June later remembered their talk as happy and upbeat, full of optimism about the future and excitement about my upcoming wedding. Laura went to bed right after the call ended. George went to wake her much later than usual the next morning, but found that she'd passed away during the night. He told everyone she had a lovely smile on her face, as if she was in the middle of a beautiful dream.

Laura was buried in a charming cemetery in Colma, the City of Souls. The town has only a little over ~~17,000~~seventeen thousand people, but ~~1.5~~one and a half million souls. It is also known as the "city of the dead" because of the many~~,~~ old cemeteries. The dead greatly outnumber the living in Colma. George lived until 1978, when he passed and was buried with Laura.

After Laura passed, June told me about a conversation she'd had with her mom about two weeks before her death. Laura said, "I want you to know that something is going to happen in a couple of weeks. Don't be scared or worry about it, but something will happen." When June remembered the conversation and told me about it, she realized Laura had known about her own death and just hadn't wanted June to be scared. Laura was not afraid and didn't want June to be afraid either.

Laura was an extraordinary woman, courageous, tenacious, and persistent. She overcame so many incredible challenges in her life, but never gave up on her family. I'm sure she considered herself quite ordinary, but what a wonderful model she was for her children and grandchildren!

My mother, June-was another exceptional woman, mother to five kids, career woman with the State of California for decades, who then had the courage to jump into a new field, managing a print shop. As if that wasn't enough, she took her small inheritance from George and started a business at age fifty-four—the first laminating business in Sacramento. Mom loved the printing community and built an excellent reputation for herself and her business, Azevedo's Laminating. She retired in 2008 (not willingly) and spent most of her time with family and friends until her death on December 10th, 2023. Those final years should have been full of joy and fun, but dementia is always a cruel surprise when it strikes.

-Now you have all the secrets and truths about Laura and her (my) family and how she lived through sixty-three turbulent years. If you are a reader, I hope this book enhanced your enjoyment for the four books in the series, and helped clear up any questions you might have had. If you are a writer with thoughts about embarking on a series of your own, I hope this book might have helped with an idea or suggestion or two that can help make your series a reality.

If you are blessed to still have grandparents, great-grandparents or other elderly relatives in your life, please talk to them, listen to their stories, treasure the moments you have left. For when they are gone, you will have lost a precious resource into your own history and your own story!

Above, June, age 15, and Laura at June's school

Patriotic June at 13, just after WWII was declared.

June and Jack's wedding day

lune and lack's first house and first car

Jack, June and baby Sharon
(author)

Above, Jack and baby Sharon by the CocaCola truck Jack drove.

On left, Jack and baby Mike
on their family car.

Above, George and Laura in 1958
Next page, George and Laura, so happy together.
He loved her and delighted in doing things to make her happy and giving her gifts.

George loved the San Francisco area and the ocean, and Laura learned to love the area too!

Laura was a terrific mother and grandmother. Here she is with June's three oldest children, baby Patrick in Laura's arms, Mike in front on the left, and Sharon (author) in front on the right

www.ingramcontent.com/pod-product-compliance
Lightning Source LLC
Chambersburg PA
CBHW061832040426
42447CB00012B/2936

* 9 7 8 1 9 4 9 1 2 5 4 2 9 *